The Israeli Guitar Book

Compiled, Edited, and Arranged by
JEFF COHEN

A step - by - step guide to playing music on the guitar.

Including:
- Standard musical notation
- Easy to read tablature
- Songs for the Holidays, Sabbath and favorite Hebrew hits.

EVANSTON PUBLIC LIBRARY
1703 ORRINGTON AVENUE
EVANSTON, ILLINOIS 60201

Tara Publications

In loving memory of my dear grandfather

ISRAEL BINSTOCK

whose spirit sings through me

FOREWORD

In writing the Israeli Guitar Book, I have utilized the notation systems and instruction methods found in the vast majority of guitar songbooks and literature.

What makes this book special, though, is that it teaches with the aid of Hebrew songs. The songs presented here are just a small sampling of the many beautiful melodies which have been composed through the ages. It is my heart-felt hope that these songs will kindle a growing appreciation for our vast Jewish heritage and will foster an identification with our precious homeland, *Eretz Yisrael*.

I must express special thanks to Rabbi Pincus Miller for introducing me to the *nachas* (supreme gratification) of playing Jewish music for and with the people who share our proud heritage.

Thanks, most of all, to my loving parents, Dorene and Eugene Cohen, for giving me everything - - and more! - - that a Jewish son needs to live a healthy, happy life.

J.C.

Jerusalem, Israel
Elul, 5743

© 1983
by
TARA PUBLICATIONS

All rights reserved. No part of this book may be reproduced in any form without permission in writing from the publisher.

PRINTED IN THE UNITED STATES OF AMERICA

Contents

HOW TO USE THIS BOOK..4
TUNING THE GUITAR: STRING NAMES AND NUMBERS 5
READING MUSIC: READING TABLATURE..6
HOW TO KEEP TIME:COUNTING MUSIC 7
HOLDING THE GUITAR:FINGER NAMES AND NUMBERS:HAND POSITIONS 8
READING THE CHORD CHART 9
HEBREW LYRICS..10
HOW TO PLAY THE MELODY..12

MUSIC SELECTIONS
1. David Melech Yisrael 13
2. Shalom Chaverim 14
3. Zum Gali Gali 15
4. Hine Ma Tov 16
5. Dayenu 17
6. Chag Purim 18
7. Ma-oz Tzur 19
8. Erev Ba 20
9. Erev Shel Shoshanim 21
10. Siman Tov 22
11. Hevenu Shalom Alechem 24
12. Od Yishama 25
13. Ose Shalom 26
14. Ya Ribon 28
15. Sisu Et Y'rushalayim 30
16. Yism'chu Hashamayim 32
17. Artza Alinu 33
18. Hatikva 34
19. Bashana Haba-a 36
20. Ele Chamda Libi 38
21. Avinu Malkenu 40
22. Rad Halaila 42
23. Eliyahu Hanavi 44
24. Hava Nagila 45

STRUM INDEX: SYMBOL EXPLANATIONS 47
RIGHT HAND POSITION-CLUSTER,ARPEGGIO AND ARPEGGIATED CLUSTER 48

HOW TO USE THIS BOOK

BEGINNING GUITAR PLAYERS

The thorough and thoughtful student will learn to play the melody by reading, counting and playing the notes of each selection. *Follow the order of the book*. Each song contains a new lesson to be learned.

ACCOMPANISTS, GUITAR PICKERS AND STRUMMERS

These songs have been arranged with fingerpicking arpeggios and strums. The pick style guitarist can easily adapt these suggested strums by sounding the bass with a pick and by strumming the Downs and Ups. The Rasguedo (Flamenco) effect can be simulated by "brushing" the pick across the strings. Please note that these accompaniment patterns are referred to as *Suggested* strums. These are by no means the only way to play these songs. After mastering all the strums, try varying the patterns by using different strums for the same song.

TEACHERS

A careful reading of the comments at the end of each selection will show the progressive order of this book. With each new song the student learns a new aspect of reading music and understanding song form.

The Israeli Guitar Book may be used as a workbook in which the student may be given such written assignments as writing the rhythm count beneath the notes.

THE STRINGS OF THE GUITAR

The guitar has six strings of different thicknesses which produce different tones. The thicker the string, the lower its sound, the thinner the string, the higher its sound.

As you hold the guitar, the thickest string should be top-most. This is the low *E string*, the sixth string of the guitar. Each string of the guitar is referred to by both a name and a number.

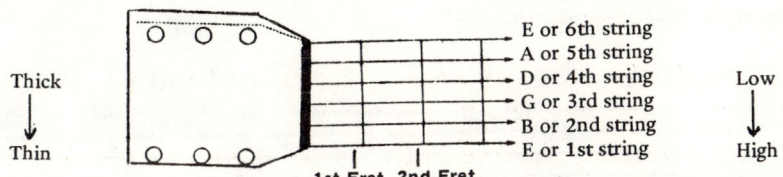

The neck of the guitar is divided by slightly raised bars called *FRETS*. The tone produced by each string can be varied by positioning a finger at different fret points. In this manner, the six strings of the guitar can produce a whole range of musical notes.

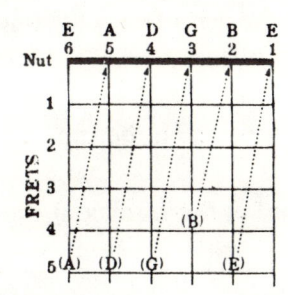

TUNING THE GUITAR

The pegs which extend from the head of the guitar are gears which increase and decrease the tension in the extended strings. The tighter the guitar string is stretched, the higher ("sharper") its sound; the looser the string, the lower ("flatter") its sound.

The guitar is tuned by turning the pegs to adjust the tones produced by the strings.

1) Place your left index finger on the E (6th) string behind the fifth fret.
2) Pluck the string with your right hand.
3) Play the A (5th) string open (unfretted). The sound produced by this string should precisely match that of the fretted 6th string. If it doesn't, tighten or loosen the 5th string until the sounds correspond.
4) Press the A (5th) string behind the 5th fret and tune the open D (4th) string to it.
5) Press the D (4th) string behind the 5th fret and tune the open G (3rd) string to it.
6) Press the G (3rd) string behind the 4th fret and tune the open B (2nd) string to it.
7) Press the B (2nd) string behind the 5th fret and tune the open E (1st) string to it.

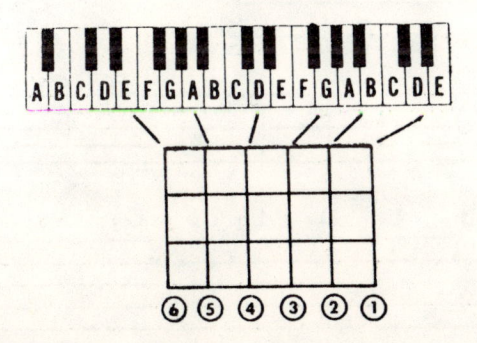

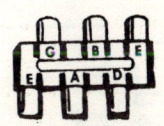

READING MUSIC

Music is written on a Staff, a series of five horizontal lines. The staff contains five lines and four spaces. Music notes can appear on any line or any space on the staff.

The musical alphabet consists of the first seven letters of the English alphabet, repeated over and over again.

   Going upwards: A B C D E F G A B ....
   Going downwards: B A G F E D C B A ....

These are the notes as they appear on the staff:

THE NOTES ON THE STAFF

These are the notes on lines: E G B D F

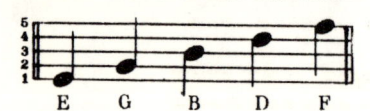

These are the notes in spaces: F A C E

When notes are too high or too low to be written on the staff, added lines called *Leger* lines are written above or below the staff.

The chart below indicates all the notes used in this book and where they can be found on the guitar.

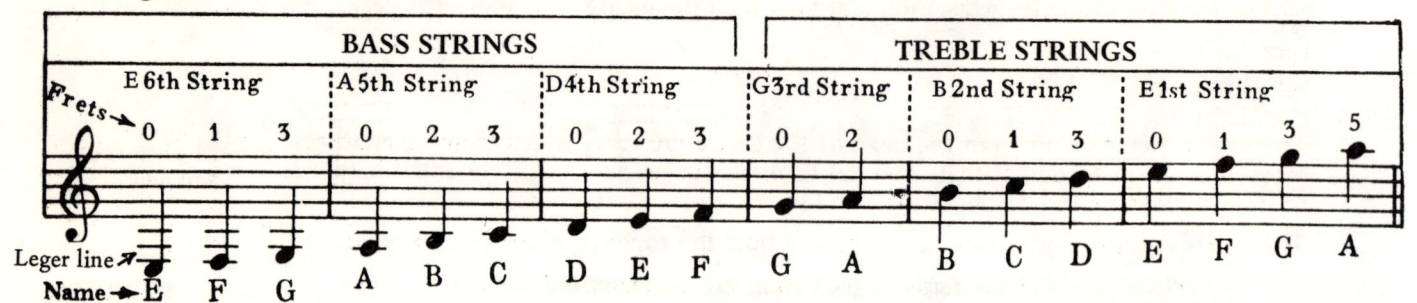

BASS STRINGS — E 6th String, A 5th String, D 4th String
TREBLE STRINGS — G 3rd String, B 2nd String, E 1st String

Names: E F G A B C D E F G A B C D E F G A

READING TABLATURE

Each line indicates a string. The top line represents the first string, second line the second string, etc. A zero means an open string, a number in the six line staff below the music indicates the fretted position, e.g. a 1 indicates the first fret of that string.

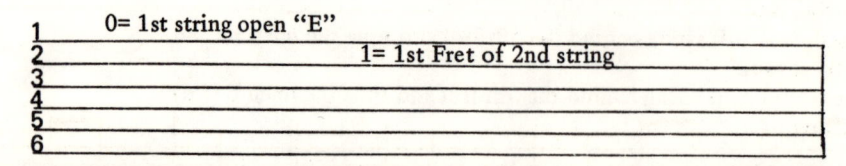

0 = 1st string open "E"
1 = 1st Fret of 2nd string

ALL NOTES USED IN THIS BOOK IN MUSIC AND TABLATURE

HOW TO KEEP TIME: COUNTING MUSIC

Counting music (keeping time) is very much like simple arithmetic. There are 5 types of notes that you will find in this book— a *whole* note gets 4 beats (1+(and) 2+3+4+)- a *half* note gets 2 beats— a *quarter* note gets 1 beat— an *eighth* note gets ½ beat (it takes 2 *eighth* notes to equal a *quarter* note or 1 beat). Towards the end of the book you will find *sixteenth* notes— four of these equal one *quarter* note (1 beat).

NOTE FORM	NOTE CHARACTER	NUMBER OF COUNTS
WHOLE	o	4
HALF	𝅗𝅥	2
QUARTER	♩	1
EIGHTH	♪ One Flag	½ 2 to one count
SIXTEENTH	𝅘𝅥𝅯 Two Flags	¼ 4 to one count

COMMON TIME

Music is divided into measures by Bar lines. The time signature found immediately to the right of the Clef indicates what kind and how many beats are found in each bar.

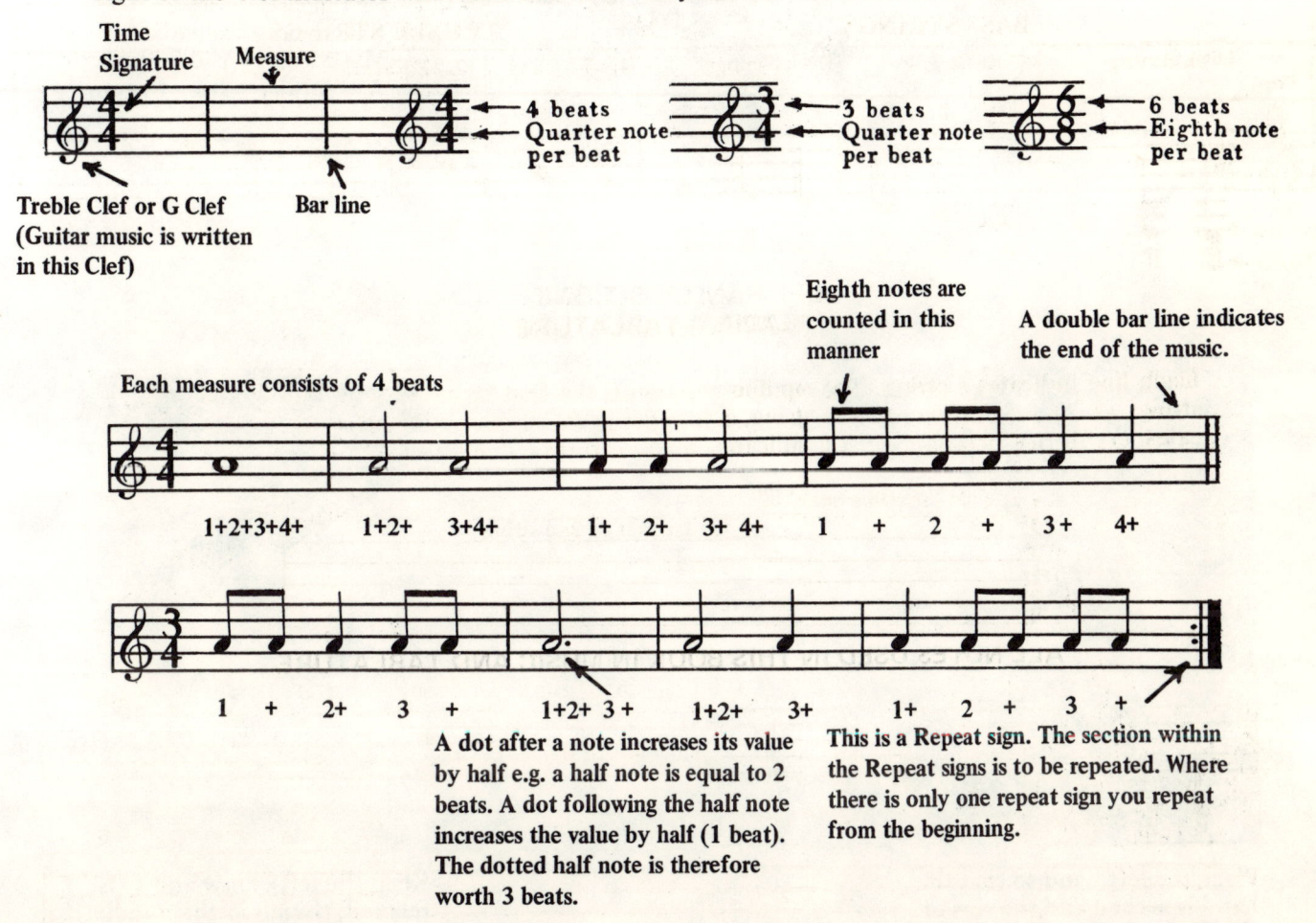

Time Signature   Measure
4/4 ← 4 beats — Quarter note per beat
3/4 ← 3 beats — Quarter note per beat
6/8 ← 6 beats — Eighth note per beat

Treble Clef or G Clef (Guitar music is written in this Clef)   Bar line

Each measure consists of 4 beats

Eighth notes are counted in this manner

A double bar line indicates the end of the music.

1+2+3+4+   1+2+ 3+4+   1+ 2+ 3+ 4+   1 + 2 + 3+ 4+

1 + 2+ 3 +   1+2+ 3 +   1+2+ 3+   1+ 2 + 3 +

A dot after a note increases its value by half e.g. a half note is equal to 2 beats. A dot following the half note increases the value by half (1 beat). The dotted half note is therefore worth 3 beats.

This is a Repeat sign. The section within the Repeat signs is to be repeated. Where there is only one repeat sign you repeat from the beginning.

HOLDING THE GUITAR

Folk Style
(Guitar on right leg)

Folk Style
(Cross right leg)

Classical

LEFT HAND

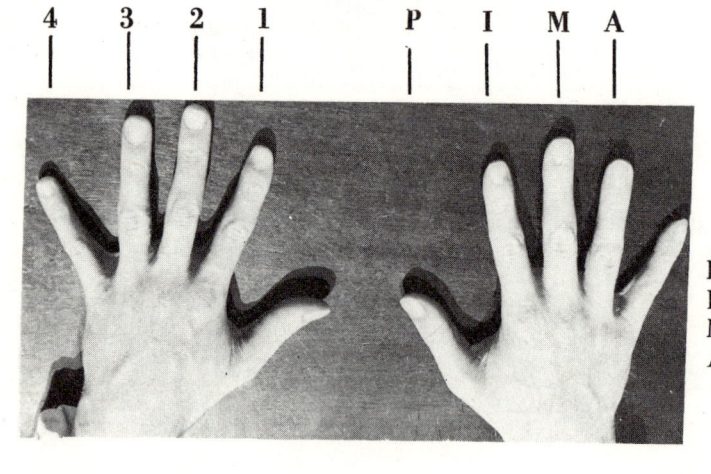

4 3 2 1   P I M A

RIGHT HAND CHART

P = Pulgar = thumb
I = Indicio = Index finger
M = Medio = Middle finger
A = Anular = Ring finger

LEFT HAND POSITIONS

Place the left hand so that the hand is arched and the tips of the fingers fall just behind the frets.

Keep the left elbow and wrist relaxed; thumb in the middle of the neck, never protruding over the edge near the strings

THIS IS A CHORD

C

X means *do not play this string*

Any string not marked by an X or a number is played *open* (unfretted).

B- Bass or Root note

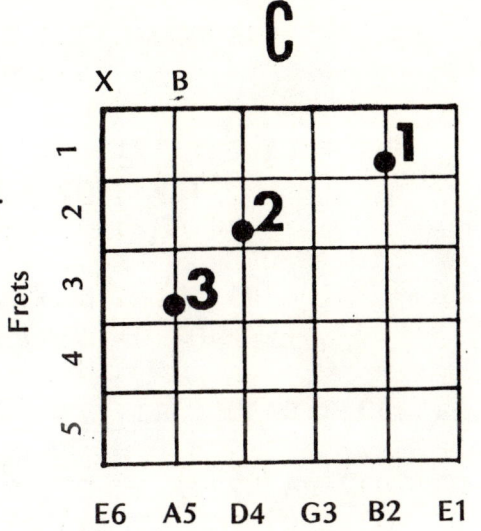

CHORDS USED IN THIS BOOK

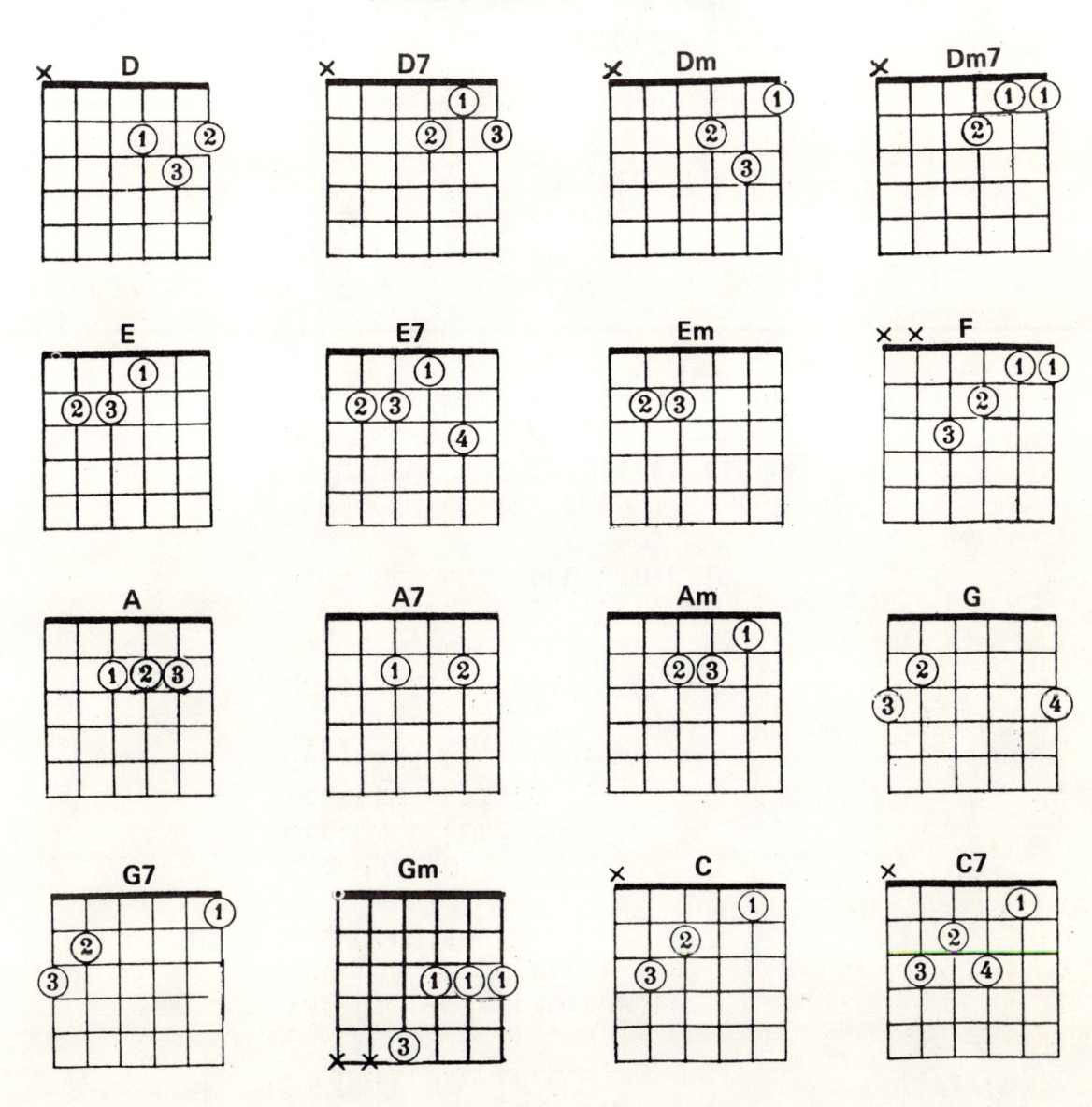

D, D7, Dm, Dm7

E, E7, Em, F

A, A7, Am, G

G7, Gm, C, C7

SONG TEXTS

PAGE No.

13   דָּוִד מֶלֶךְ יִשְׂרָאֵל חַי וְקַיָּם

14   שָׁלוֹם חֲבֵרִים לְהִתְרָאוֹת
         שָׁלוֹם שָׁלוֹם

15   זוּם גָּלִי – גָּלִי זוּם גָּלִי – גָּלִי
         הֶחָלוּץ לְמַעַן עֲבוֹדָה
         עֲבוֹדָה לְמַעַן הֶחָלוּץ

16   הִנֵּה מַה טוֹב וּמַה נָּעִים
         שֶׁבֶת אַחִים גַּם יָחַד

17   אִלּוּ הוֹצִיאָנוּ מִמִּצְרַיִם דַּיֵּינוּ

18   חַג פּוּרִים חַג גָּדוֹל הוּא לַיְּהוּדִים
         מַסֵּכוֹת רַעֲשָׁנִים זְמִירוֹת וְרִקּוּדִים
         הָבָה נַרְעִישָׁה רַשׁ רַשׁ רַשׁ בָּרַעֲשָׁנִים

19   מָעוֹז צוּר יְשׁוּעָתִי לְךָ נָאֶה לְשַׁבֵּחַ
         תִּכּוֹן בֵּית תְּפִלָּתִי וְשָׁם תּוֹדָה נְזַבֵּחַ
         לְעֵת תָּכִין מַטְבֵּחַ מִצָּר הַמְנַבֵּחַ
         אָז אֶגְמוֹר בְּשִׁיר מִזְמוֹר חֲנֻכַּת הַמִּזְבֵּחַ

20   שׁוּב הָעֵדֶר נוֹדֵד בִּמְבוֹאוֹת הַכְּפָר
         וְעוֹלֶה הָאָבָק מִשְּׁבִילֵי עָפָר
         וְהַרְחֵק עוֹד צֶמֶד עֲנָבָלִים
         מְלַוֶּה אֶת מַשַּׁק הַצְּלָלִים
         עֶרֶב בָּא עֶרֶב בָּא

21   עֶרֶב שֶׁל שׁוֹשַׁנִּים נֵצֵא נָא אֶל הַבֻּסְתָּן
         מוֹר בְּשָׂמִים וּלְבוֹנָה לְרַגְלֵךְ מִפְתָּן
         לַיְלָה יוֹרֵד לְאַט וְרוּחַ שׁוֹשָׁן נוֹשְׁבָה
         הָבָה אֶלְחַשׁ לָךְ שִׁיר בַּלָּאט זֶמֶר שֶׁל אַהֲבָה

22   סִימָן טוֹב וּמַזָּל טוֹב יְהֵא לָנוּ
         וּלְכָל יִשְׂרָאֵל

24   הֲבֵאנוּ שָׁלוֹם עֲלֵיכֶם

25   עוֹד יִשָּׁמַע בְּעָרֵי יְהוּדָה
         וּבְחוּצוֹת יְרוּשָׁלַיִם
         קוֹל שָׂשׂוֹן וְקוֹל שִׂמְחָה
         קוֹל חָתָן וְקוֹל כַּלָּה

26   עוֹשֶׂה שָׁלוֹם בִּמְרוֹמָיו
         הוּא יַעֲשֶׂה שָׁלוֹם עָלֵינוּ
         וְעַל כָּל יִשְׂרָאֵל וְאִמְרוּ אָמֵן

28   יָהּ רִבּוֹן עָלַם וְעָלְמַיָּא
         אַנְתְּ הוּא מַלְכָּא מֶלֶךְ מַלְכַיָּא
         עוֹבַד גְּבוּרְתֵּךְ וְתִמְהַיָּא
         שְׁפַר קָדָמָךְ לְהַחֲוָיָה

SONG TEXTS

30
שִׁישׂוּ אֶת יְרוּשָׁלַיִם גִּילוּ בָהּ
גִּילוּ בָהּ כָּל אוֹהֲבֶיהָ
עַל חוֹמוֹתַיִךְ עִיר דָּוִד
הִפְקַדְתִּי שׁוֹמְרִים
כָּל הַיּוֹם וְכָל הַלַּיְלָה

32
יִשְׂמְחוּ הַשָּׁמַיִם וְתָגֵל הָאָרֶץ
יִרְעַם הַיָּם וּמְלֹאוֹ

33
אַרְצָה עָלִינוּ
כְּבָר חָרַשְׁנוּ וְגַם זָרַעְנוּ
אֲבָל עוֹד לֹא קָצַרְנוּ

34
כָּל עוֹד בַּלֵּבָב פְּנִימָה
נֶפֶשׁ יְהוּדִי הוֹמִיָּה
וּלְפַאֲתֵי מִזְרָח קָדִימָה
עַיִן לְצִיּוֹן צוֹפִיָּה
עוֹד לֹא אָבְדָה תִּקְוָתֵנוּ
הַתִּקְוָה בַּת שְׁנוֹת אַלְפַּיִם
לִהְיוֹת עַם חָפְשִׁי בְּאַרְצֵנוּ
אֶרֶץ צִיּוֹן וִירוּשָׁלַיִם

36
בַּשָּׁנָה הַבָּאָה נֵשֵׁב עַל הַמִּרְפֶּסֶת
וְנִסְפֹּר צִפֳּרִים נוֹדְדוֹת
יְלָדִים בְּחֻפְשָׁה יְשַׂחֲקוּ תּוֹפֶסֶת
בֵּין הַבַּיִת לְבֵין הַשָּׂדוֹת
עוֹד תִּרְאֶה עוֹד תִּרְאֶה
כַּמָּה טוֹב יִהְיֶה
בַּשָּׁנָה הַבָּאָה

38
אַיֶּלֶת חֶמְדָּה לִבִּי
וְחוּשָׁה נָא וְעַל תִּתְעַלֵּם

40
אָבִינוּ מַלְכֵּנוּ חָנֵּנוּ וַעֲנֵנוּ
כִּי אֵין בָּנוּ מַעֲשִׂים
עֲשֵׂה עִמָּנוּ צְדָקָה
וָחֶסֶד וְהוֹשִׁיעֵנוּ

42
רַד הַלַּיְלָה רַב שִׁירֵנוּ הַבּוֹקֵעַ לַשָּׁמַיִם
שׁוּבִי שׁוּבִי הוֹרָתֵנוּ מְחֻדֶּשֶׁת שִׁבְעָתַיִם
שׁוּבִי שׁוּבִי וְנָסֹב כִּי דַרְכֵּנוּ אֵין לָהּ סוֹף
כִּי עוֹד נִמְשֶׁכֶת הַשַּׁלְשֶׁלֶת
כִּי לִבֵּנוּ לֵב אֶחָד מֵעוֹלָם וְעֲדֵי עַד
כִּי עוֹד נִמְשֶׁכֶת הַשַּׁרְשֶׁרֶת

44
אֵלִיָּהוּ הַנָּבִיא אֵלִיָּהוּ הַתִּשְׁבִּי
אֵלִיָּהוּ הַגִּלְעָדִי
בִּמְהֵרָה בְיָמֵינוּ יָבֹא אֵלֵינוּ
עִם מָשִׁיחַ בֶּן דָּוִד

45
הָבָה נָגִילָה וְנִשְׂמְחָה
עוּרוּ אַחִים בְּלֵב שָׂמֵחַ

HOW TO PLAY THE MELODY

Here are the first 4 measures of David Melech Yisrael. The first thing to do is to look at the first note and say its name. If you need to, look at the chart on page 6. The tablature underneath the staff tells you on which string and which fret (if not open) the note can be found. The next step is to see which finger to use to hold down the note. The little numer to the left of the note tells you which finger to use.

In the first line we see that G is played "open" - 0. E is played with your second finger-2. A is played with your second finger-2, F is played with your third finger-3, D is played "open"-0.

After you have identified the name of the note, where it is on the guitar and which finger holds down the note you go on to the next step. *Count out loud* as you play the note and *tap your foot to keep the beat.* All of the melodies *may be played with a guitar pick or fingers and/or thumb.* Because all the notes of David Melech Yisrael are on the 3rd, 4th and 5th strings I recommend using your thumb to pluck the strings.

DAVID MELECH YISRAËL

STEPS IN LEARNING A SONG

1. Know the names of the notes.
2. Know where they are found on the guitar.
3. Look at the fingering numbers. They will indicate which finger holds down the note.
4. Write the rhythm (counting numbers) underneath the notes.
5. *Count out loud, keep the beat* by tapping your foot and play!

Suggested Strum Cluster: Thumb & Index

	B	Alt
C	5	4
F	4	
G	6	4
G7	6	4

SHALOM CHAVËRIM

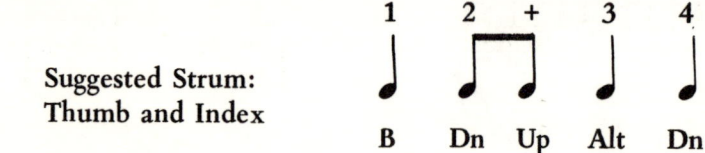

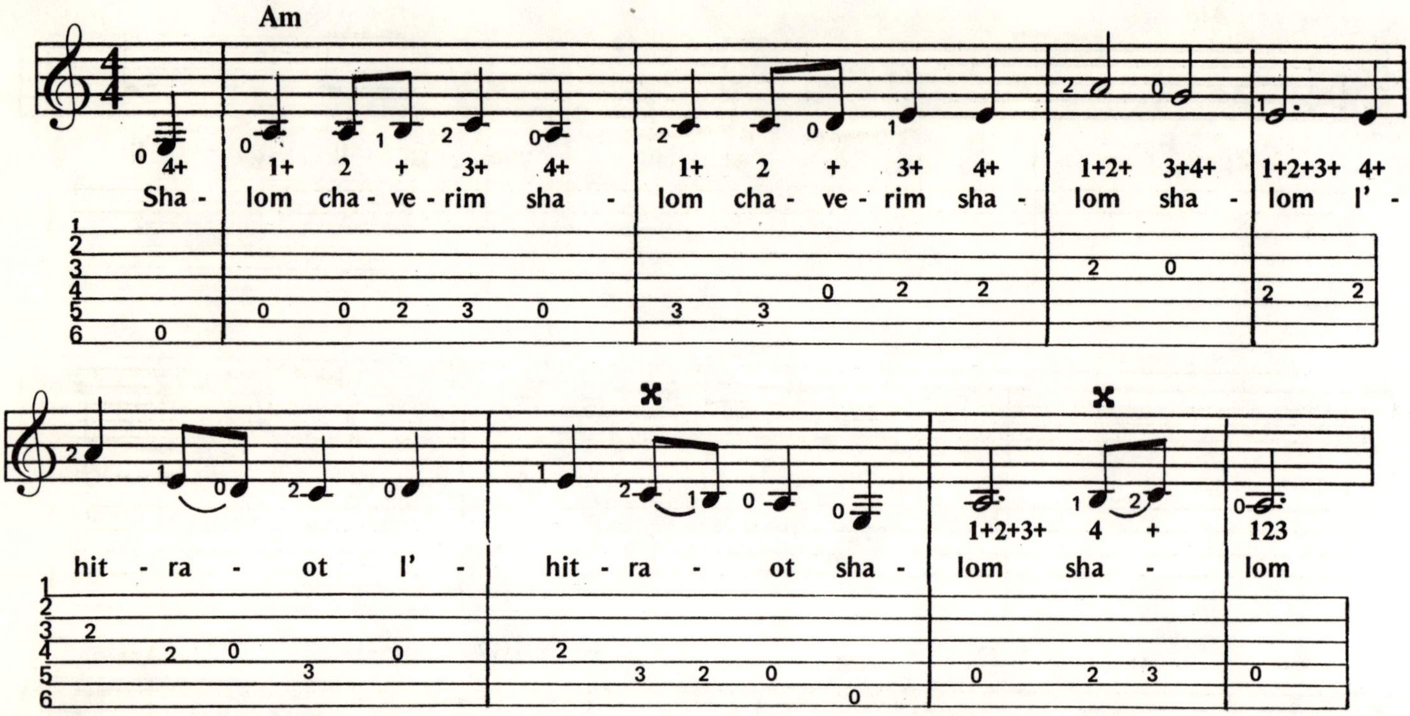
Am
4+ 1+ 2 + 3+ 4+ 1+ 2 + 3+ 4+ 1+2+ 3+4+ 1+2+3+ 4+
Sha - lom cha - ve - rim sha - lom cha - ve - rim sha - lom sha - lom l' -
hit - ra - ot l' - hit - ra - ot sha - lom sha - lom
1+2+3+ 4 + 123

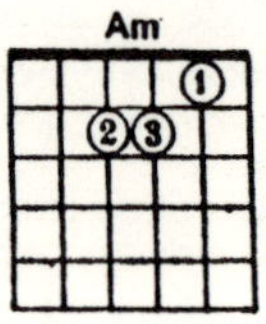
Am

Am - Bass-5
Alt - 4

Suggested Strum:
Thumb and Index

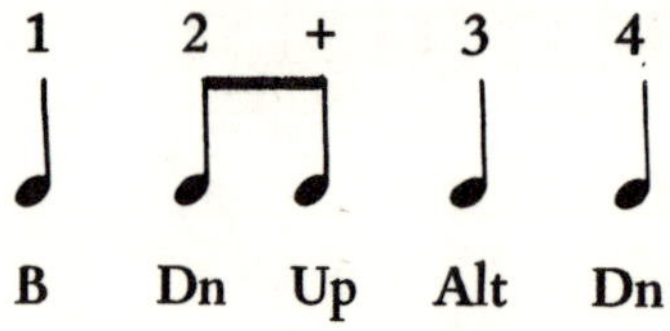
1 2 + 3 4
B Dn Up Alt Dn

Shalom Chaverim begins on the 4th beat. I have written out the beginning and ending rhythm count. Fill in all other numbers underneath the notes. Count out loud and pay close attention to the left hand fingering. If you find a particular measure or a group of notes that give you difficulty- practice *just those notes* until they become easier to play and then go back and fit them in with the rest of the song. It may help to memorize trouble spots so that you can give your full attention to your fingers without looking at the music. Use your thumb for this song. ✖ ‿ appears when two or more notes are sung on the same syllable.

ZUM GALI

Am
Zum ga - li ga - li ga - li zum ga - li ga - li
Am
zum ga - li ga - li ga - li zum ga - li ga - li he - cha -
Am Dm Am E7 Am
lutz l' - ma'm a - vo - da a - vo - da l' - ma'n he - cha - lutz

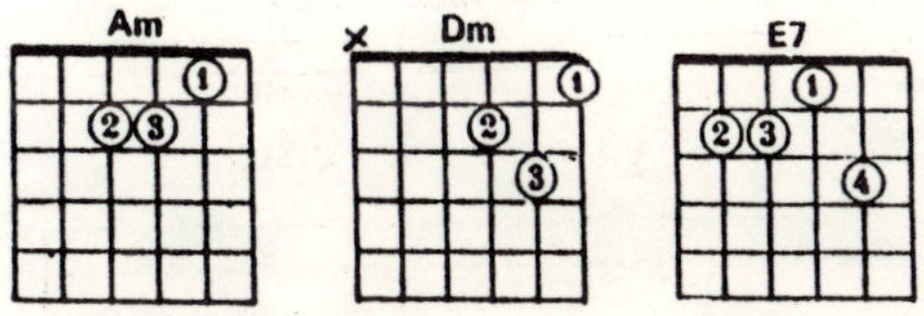
Am
Dm
E7

Suggested Strum Cluster

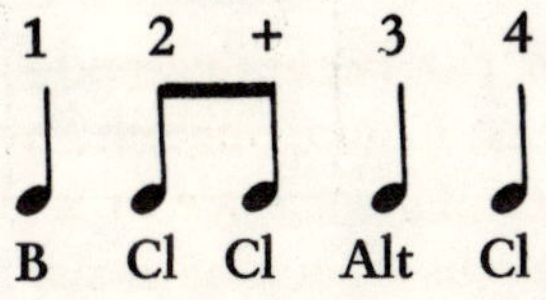
1 2 + 3 4
B Cl Cl Alt Cl

	B	Alt
Am	5	4
Dm	4	5
E7	6	4

The melody for Zum Gali Gali falls on the 1st 4 strings. Except for the low E note (4th string) play all the notes with your I + M fingers. Alternate between them I,M-I, M, I, M, etc. We have our first Quarter note rest. Fill in the rest of the rhythm numbers.

HINĒ MA TOV

Our first song in 3/4 time. Remember to count 3 beats per measure (1 2 3). It is usually a good idea to "accent" the 1st beat in 3/4 - <u>one</u> two three. Notice the repeat sign after measure 8 :||. You go back to the beginning and play the whole way through until the end.

DAYËNU

[Sheet music with guitar tablature in 4/4 time]

Lyrics under the staves:
I - lu ho - tzi ho - tzi - a - nu ho - tzi - a - nu mi - mitz - ra - yim
ho - tzi - a - nu mi - mitz - ra - yim da - yë - nu
da da yë - nu___ da da - yë - nu___ da da - yë - nu da -
(1.) ye - nu da - yë - nu da - yë - nu
(2.) yë - nu da - yë - nu

Chords used: C, G, G7

Chords	B	Alt
C	5	4
F	4	
G	6	4

Suggested Strum Cluster: 1+ 2+ 3+ 4+ B C1 A C1 B C1 A C1

Dayenu introduces our first repeat with two different endings. You play all the way through ending number 1 and then go back to the repeat sign 𝄆 at the beginning of measure number 9 ✘. You play from there until the first ending (you do not play that again). Play the second ending and that is the end of the song. Measure 5 ✘ introduces our first "syncopated rhythm." This means that the beat falls on the weaker count (+). I have shown you how to count this measure. You should have no trouble filling in the rest. Remember! Count out loud and keep a steady beat (1 2 3 4) with your foot. After you have counted and played a song many times you may want to try and <u>hum</u> the melody as you play it. The next step is to sing the words. Good luck! Play notes on the first 3 strings with I + M alternating; notes on the 4th and 5th with the thumb.

CHAG PURIM

Notice the sharp sign between the G Clef and the time signature. It is on the line on which the F note falls. This means that F is sharp. Wherever F is indicated ✘ you play F♯. To make a note sharp you move up one fret. In this case F would normally be on the 4th string 3rd fret— F♯ is found on the fourth string 4th fret.

The rhythm and song form are very easy. See if you can count 1 2 3 4 for those measures that don't have eighth notes. Count 1 + 2 + 3 + 4 + for those measures that do have eighth notes. You will have to keep a good steady beat with your foot.

MA-OZ TZUR

(Sheet music with guitar tablature and chord diagrams)

Lyrics beneath the staves:

Ma - oz tzur y' - shu - a - ti l' - cha na - e l' - sha -
ti - kon bët t' - fi - la - ti v' - sham to - da n' - za -
bë - ach   bë - ach l' - ët ta - chin mat - bë - ach
mi - tzar ham - na - bë - ach   az eg - mor b' -
shir miz - mor cha - nu - kat ha - miz - bë - ach

Rhythm markings under third-to-last measure: 1+2 + 3+4 +

Chord diagrams shown: G, C, D, Am

Suggested Strum: Thumb Strum — Dn Dn Up Dn Dn Up (1 2 + 3 4 +)

	B	Alt
G	6	4
C	5	4
D	4	

✱ F is sharp through this entire song. Normally the higher F is played on the first fret of the first string. F♯ is found on the 2nd fret of the 1st string.

In this selection we have dotted quarter notes. They count for a beat and a half. The rhythm has been written underneath the third measure from the end. It might be helpful to practice clapping or tapping the rhythm of the measures with the dotted quarters. Be sure to keep a steady beat with your foot.

EREV BA

Suggested Strum: Arpeggio

	B	Alt
C	5	4
Dm	4	5
G	6	4
A	5	4
Am	5	4
G7	6	4

There is nothing new here. You should be able to write the rhythm for this song by yourself. If you have any difficulty, review the songs you've already learned.

EREV SHEL SHOSHANIM

Erev shel shoshanim nëtzë na el habustan
mor b'samim u-l'vona l'rag-lëch miftan
laila yorëd l'at v'ru-ach shoshan noshva
hava el-chash lach shir ba-lat zemer shel ahava

Suggested Strum: Arpeggio

	B	Alt
Am	5	4
D	4	
Dm	4	
G	6	
Em	6	

There are no new forms with this song.

SIMAN TOV

Suggested Strum:
Thumb & Index

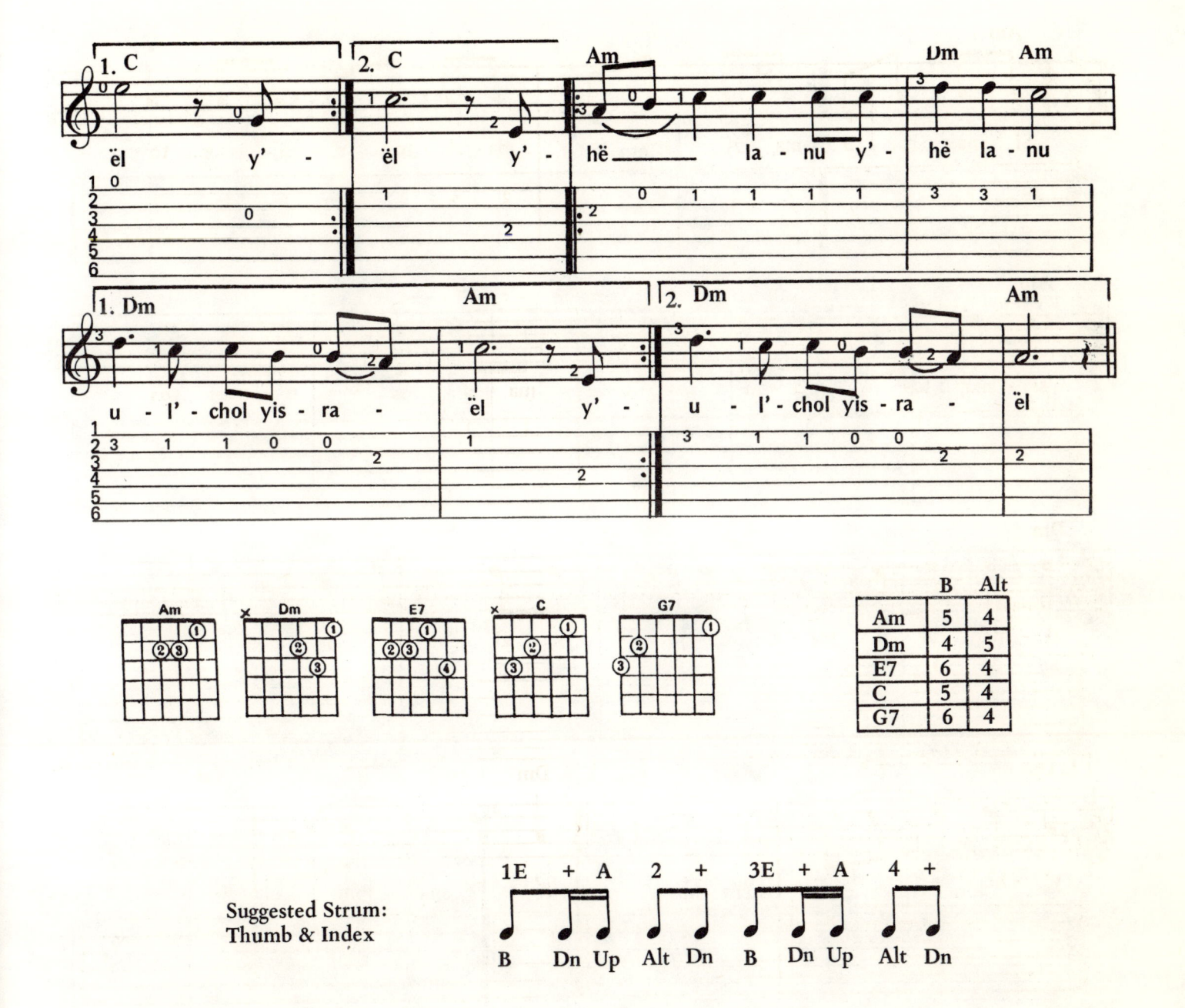

	B	Alt
Am	5	4
Dm	4	5
E7	6	4
C	5	4
G7	6	4

You should encounter no new challenges in the rhythm of Siman Tov. The form of the song is divided into three sections. Play through the 1st ending and then go back and play up to the first ending, skipping it and play the 2nd ending. Continue with the remainder of the song through the first ending and return to the beginning of the second part. Repeat and finish the song with the second ending in place of the first ending.

HËVËNU SHALOM

I hope that you have been writing out the rhythm underneath all the songs and counting out loud as you play. The entire rhythm of this song has been written out. In measure 5 at ✘ we have our first high "A" note. It is played with the 4th finger on the 5th fret of the first string.

	B	Alt
Dm	4	5
Am	5	4
E7	6	4
A7	5	4
F	6	4

OD YISHAMA

Suggested Strum: Thumb & Index

We have our first eighth note rest. ꝰ. It falls on the first beat of measure 11 ✖.
It might help you to stomp your foot on the 1st beat to get the *feel* of this *syncopation*. This song is in 2/4 time. Count two beats per measure.

OSE SHALOM

Suggested Strum:
Arpegiated Cluster

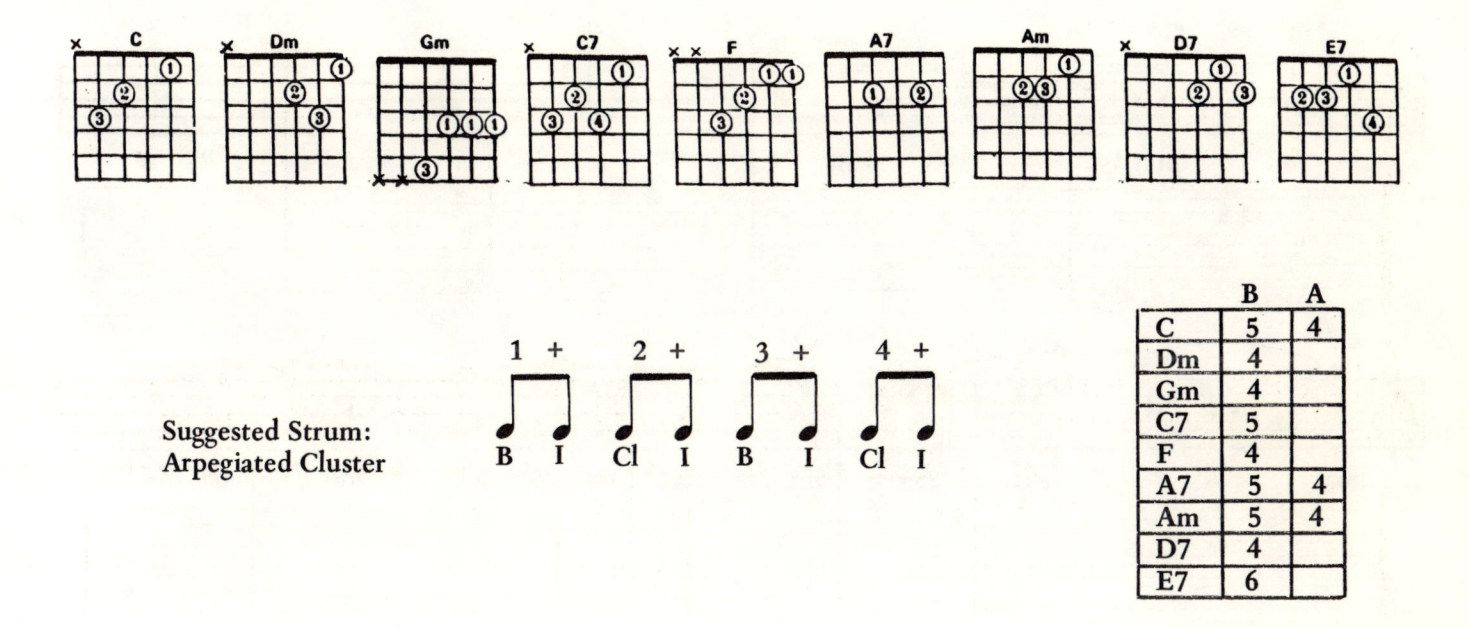

1 + 2 + 3 + 4 +
B I Cl I B I Cl I

	B	A
C	5	4
Dm	4	
Gm	4	
C7	5	
F	4	
A7	5	4
Am	5	4
D7	4	
E7	6	

When looking at a new song, the first thing you should do is to check and see if there are any ♯ (sharps) or ♭ (flats) between the clef and the time signature. In Ose Shalom, B is flat. B♭ is on the third string, third fret.

In the third measure from the end ✖ and the last measure we have our first "natural" sign ♮. <u>For this one note only we play B natural.</u>

The form of this song is once through the 1st ending; then once through using the second ending. After the second ending, play through until the end and then go back to the sign 𝄋 and play from this point using the 2nd ending. Ose Shalom should begin slowly and then build in speed in the second part, very fast for the third part and then return to the speed of the second part.

YA RIBON

29

	B	Alt
C	5	
Am	5	4
F	4	
G7	6	
A7	5	4
Dm	4	5
E7	6	
G	6	

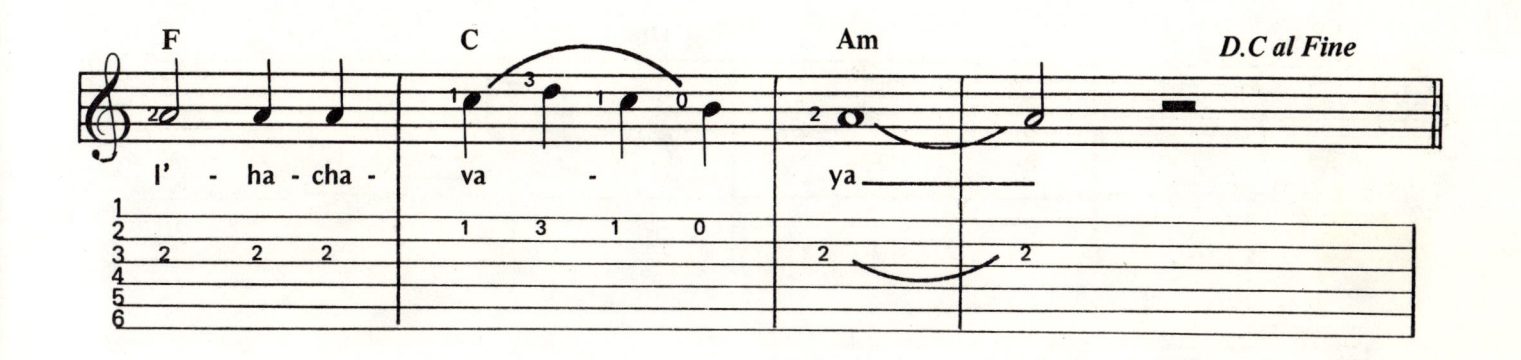

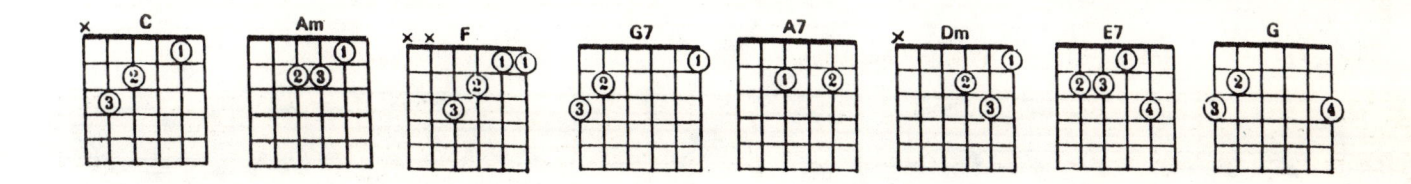

Suggested Strum:
Arpeggiated Cluster

1 2 3 4
B I Cl I

Ya Ribon uses the notes on the high E string more than any other song in the book. Be sure to pay close attention to the left hand fingering numbers. *D.C. al Fine* means go back to the beginning and play until the *Fine*. In the 19th measure I have written out the rhythm for you 1 2 3+ 4+ ✘. As you develop more of a feeling of the beat it is more efficient to count this way— using +'s only when necessary. If you are not ready to count this way, feel free to write them in. Everyone has differing levels of progress as well as different strong and weak areas.

SISU ET Y'RUSHALAYIM

Si - su et y' - ru - sha - la - yim gi - lu va gi - lu va kol o - ha - ve - ha kol o - ha - ve - ha si - su et y' - ru - sha - la - yim gi - lu va gi - lu va kol o - ha - ve - ha o - ha - ve - ha ve - ha al cho - mo - ta - yich ir da - vid hif - ka - d'ti shom - rim kol ha - yom v' - chol ha - lai - la al

31

cho - mo - ta - yich   ir   da - vid   hif - ka - d' - ti   shom - rim

kol   ha - yom___   v' - chol   ha - lai - la   kol___   ha - lai - la

D.C. al Fine

Suggested Strum:
Flamenco

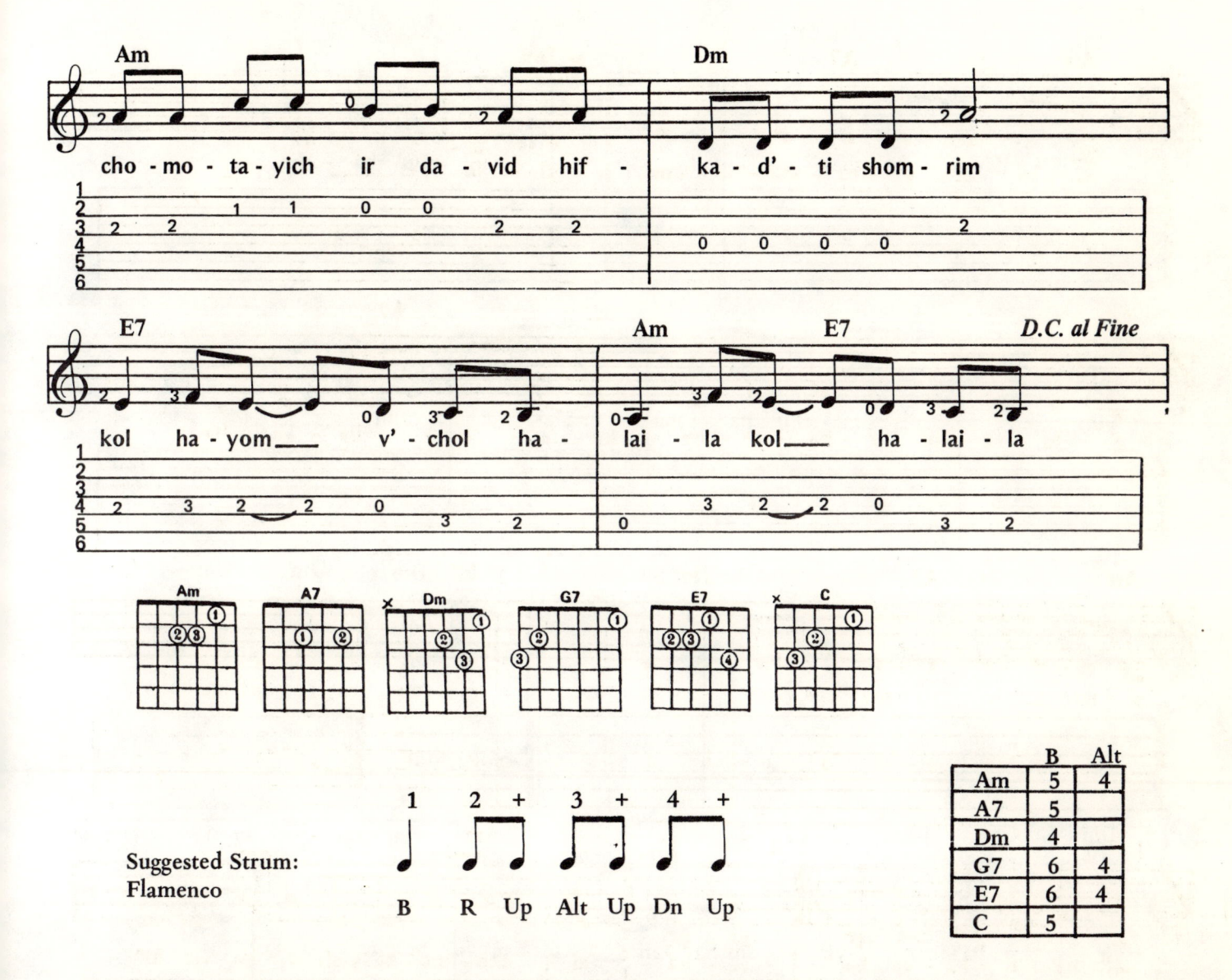

	B	Alt
Am	5	4
A7	5	
Dm	4	
G7	6	4
E7	6	4
C	5	

You will want to pay special attention to syncopation (e.g. second measure 𝄪).

D.C. al Fine means go back to the beginning and play the first section with the repeats until the *Fine* marking.

We have another accidental, five measures from the end- G♯. An accidental stays in effect for the entire measure. The second G, therefore is also played as G .

YISM'CHU HASHAMAYIM

Yis-m'-chu ha-sha-ma-yim yis-m'-chu ha-sha-ma-yim yis-m'-chu ha-sha-ma-yim v'-ta-gël ha-a-retz a-retz yir-am ha-yam yir-am ha-yam yir-am ha-yam u-m'-lo-o lo-o

	B	Alt
Dm	4	5
A7	5	4
F	4	5
Gm	4	4
C7	5	4

0 = open

Suggested Strum Cluster: 1 + 2 + 3 + 4 +
B Cl Alt Cl B Cl Alt Cl

B is flat (3rd string, 3rd fret) throughout the entire song. Play part one through the 1st ending. Go back to the beginning and play once again with the second ending, (do not play the first ending 1.). Do the same thing with the second half of the song.

ARTSA ALINU

Ar-tza a-li-nu, ar-tza a-li-nu, ar-tza a-li-nu, k'var cha-rash-nu v'-gam za-ra-nu, k'var cha-rash-nu v'-gam za-ra-nu a-val od lo ka-tzar-nu, a-val od lo ka-tzar-nu.

	B	Alt
Dm	4	5
F	4	
Gm	4	0
A7	5	
Am	5	

Suggested Strum Cluster: 1 +2 + 3 4 — B Cl Cl Alt Cl

This song has a "syncopated" melody. The rhythm has been written out for the first measure. B is flat throughout the entire song.

HATIKVA

Kol__ od ba-lë-vav p'ni-ma ne-fesh y'-hu-di
ho-mi-a ul'-fa-të miz-rach ka-di-ma
a-yin l'-tzi-yon tzo-fi-a od lo av-da
tik-va-të-nu ha-tik-va bat shnot al-pa-yim
li-yot am chof-shi b'-ar-tzë-nu

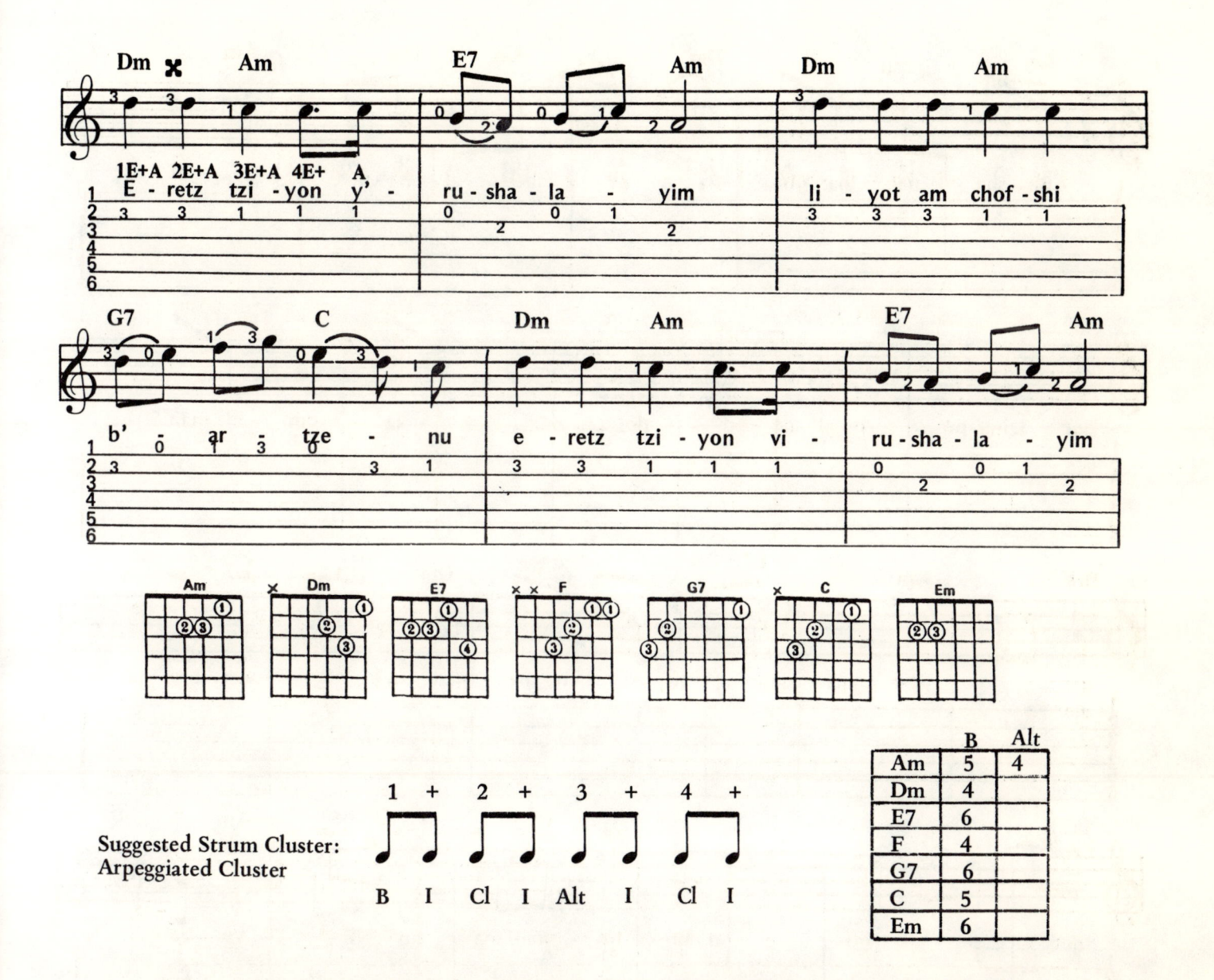

Six measures from the end we have our first dotted 8th note + 16th note. In order to count and play this figuration we must make another subdivision of the beat. When we count 1+ 2+ 3+ 4+ we are breaking the beat in half, two 8th notes = 1 quarter note. It takes four 16th notes to equal one quarter note. To break the quarter note down to four 16th's we can count 1E+A 2E+A etc. (We pronounce this *one-ee-and-ah*). To play the dotted 8th note we must place three quarters of the beat on this note and the last quarter of the beat on the 16th e.g.

1E+ A

BASHANA HABA-A

37

tov yi - ye ba - sha - na ba - sha - na ha - ba - a

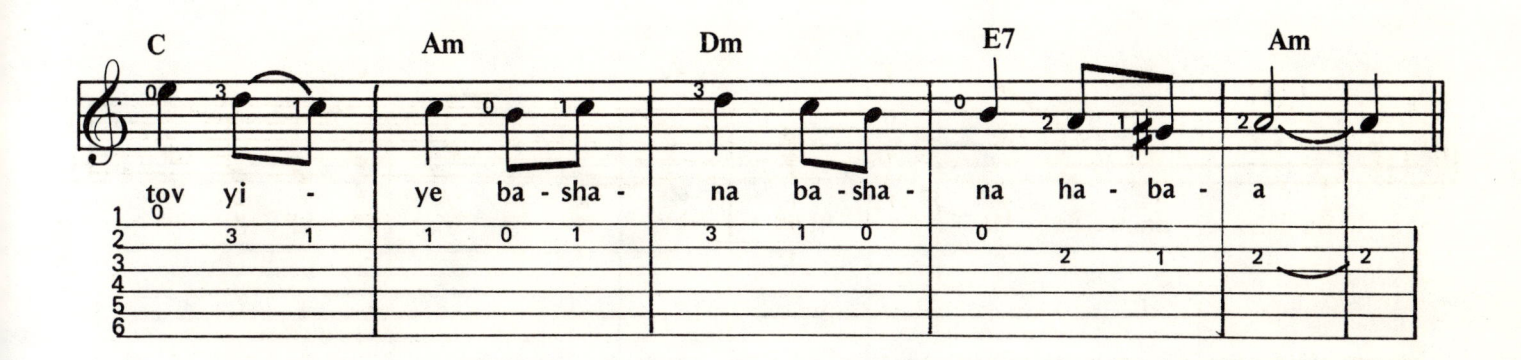

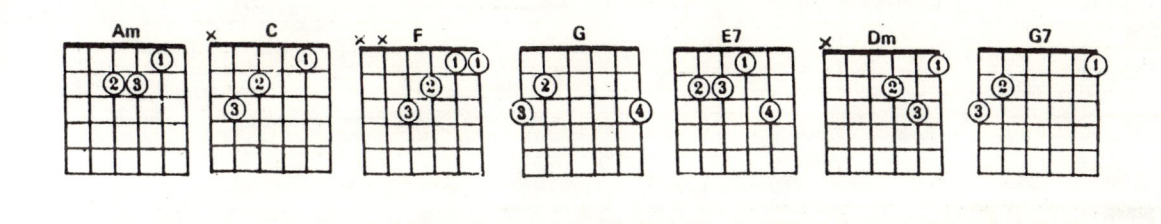

	B	Alt
Am	5	4
C	5	4
F	4	5
G	6	4
E7	6	4
Dm	4	5
G7	6	4

Suggested Strum
Flamenco

B R Up Alt Up Dn Up

ËLE CHAMDA LIBI

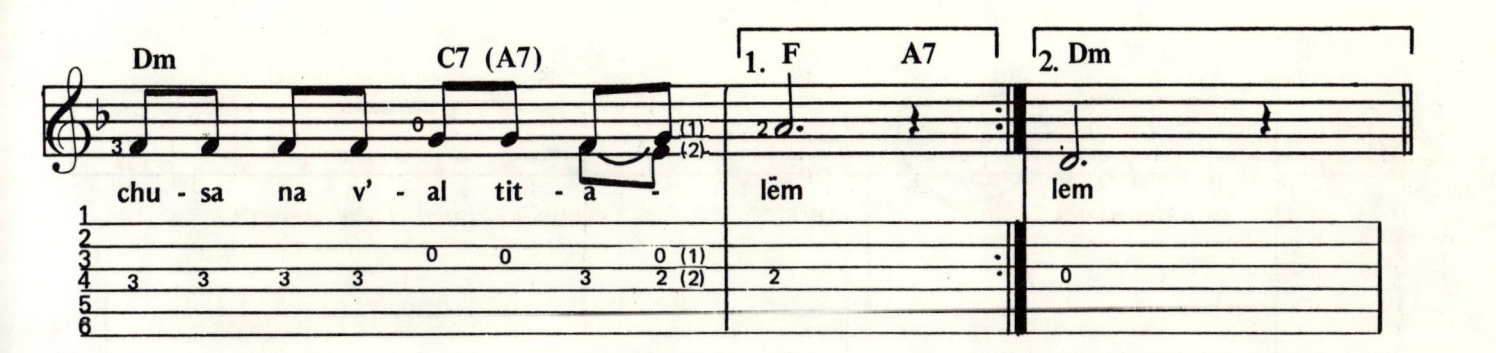

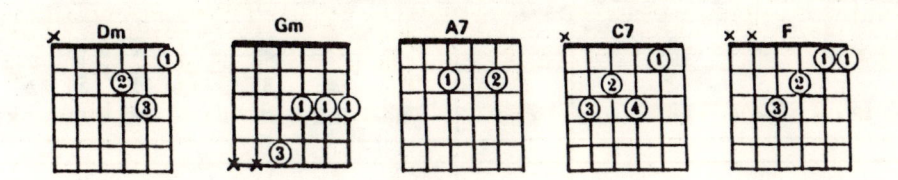

39

lyrics: chu - sa na v' - al tit - a - lēm / lem

Suggested Strum Cluster: 1 + 2 + 3 + 4 +
B Cl Alt Cl B Cl Alt Cl

	B	A
Dm	4	5
Gm	4	4⁰
A7	5	4
C7	5	4
F	4	5

AVINU MALKËNU

(sheet music: measures with lyrics "vi-nu mal-kë-nu ___ a- vi-nu mal-kë-nu ___" with chords E, Dm, E, Dm, E and tablature below)

(chord diagrams: E, Dm (x), Am)

	B	A
E	6	4
Dm	4	5
Am	5	4

Suggested Strum Cluster:

```
 1  2  3   4  5  6
 B  Cl Cl  Alt Cl Cl
```

Avinu Malkenu is our first and only song in $\frac{6}{8}$ time. An eighth note counts as 1 beat. The best way to count in $\frac{6}{8}$ time is 1 2 3,4 5 6, 1 2 3,4 5 6. The accents seem to fall naturally on the 1st and 4th beats dividing a measure into two groups of 3 notes. I have written the rhythm except for the empty places that you should be able to fill in. In measures 3 and 6 I have counted the rhythm for you. Feel free to use either of these counts (whichever you find easier). This is your book!

RAD HALAILA

43

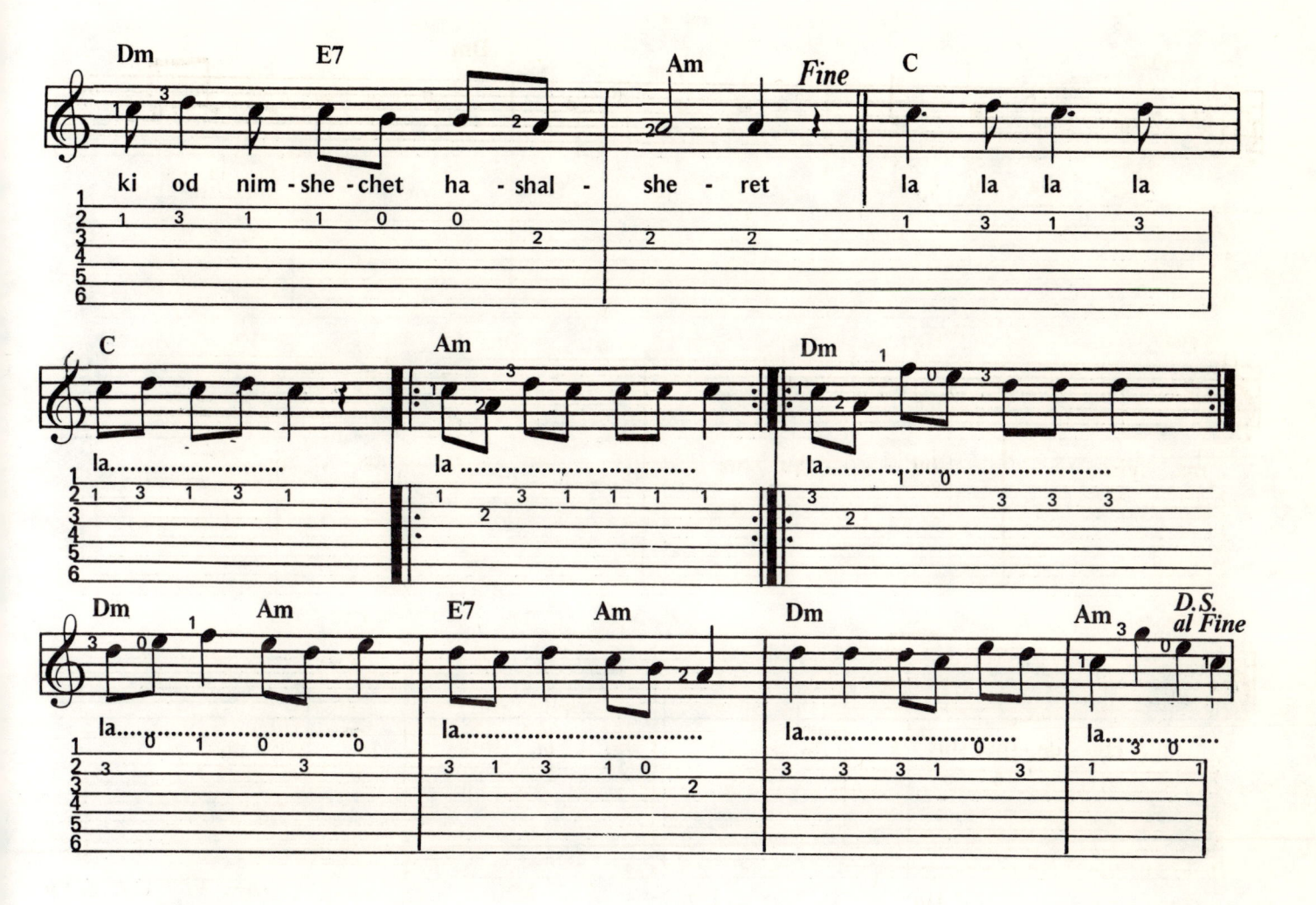

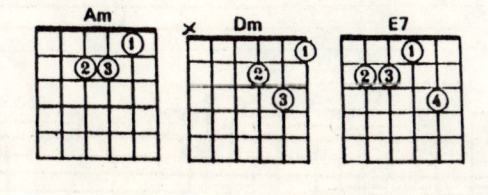

ki od nim-she-chet ha-shal-she-ret la la la la la...... la......... la......... la....... la........ la........ la........

	B	Alt
Am	5	4
Dm	4	5
E7	6	4

Suggested Strum:
Flamenco

B R Up Alt Up Dn Up

ËLIYAHU HANAVI

(sheet music with guitar tablature)

Lyrics under staves:
Ë - li - ya - hu ha - na - vi Ë - li - ya - hu ha - tish - bi
E - li - ya - hu E - li - ya - hu Ë - li - ya - hu ha - gil - a - di
bim - hë - ra v' - ya - më - nu ya - vo ë - lë - nu
im ma - shi - ach ben da - vid im ma - shi - ach ben da - vid

Chord diagrams: E7, Am, E, F, C, Dm

	B
E7	6
Am	5
E	6
F	4
C	5
Dm	4

Suggested Strum:
Thumb Strum

1 2 3
Dn Dn Dn

This song is in 3/4 time. Remember to count 3 beats per measure. In measure 7 ✘ I have written out the rhythm. You should be able to complete the remainder of the rhythm. Practice slowly at first until counting and playing seem easy and natural at which time you can play a little faster. *D.C. al Fine* — play until the end and then return to the beginning until the *Fine*

HAVA NAGILA

*These are accent marks.
The notes get a special emphasis.

	B	Alt
E	6	4
Am	5	4
Dm	4	5

Suggested Strum Cluster:

B Cl Alt Cl B Cl Alt Cl

STRUM INDEX

SYMBOL EXPLANATIONS

B- Bass (root note of the chord) played with *P* (thumb).
Alt- Alternate bass note played with *P* when holding down the notes for the Am chord, the bass is played on the 5th string. The Alternate bass is on the 4th string.

	B	Alt
Am	5	4

Dn - Down Stroke - with the exceptions of *Eliyahu Hanavi* and *Ma-oz Tzur*.* The index finger flicks down across the strings, from the lower sounding strings through the highest sounding.
Up - Up Stroke - The index finger flicks "up" the strings from the highest sounding strings through the string just before the bass note.

The flicking motion of the index finger is accomplished by bending the finger from the knuckle and making a snapping (flicking motion) outwards, away from the palm, striking the strings with the top of the nail for the down stroke; In towards your palm, striking the strings with the underside of the nail for the Up stroke.

* *Eliyahu Hanavi* and *Ma-oz Tzur* are played exclusively with the thumb.
Dn - Thumb brushes down from the bass note through the 1st string.
Up - Thumb sweeps back up the strings to the string preceeding the bass note.

Cl - Cluster - I, M, A, Fingers pull the 1st, 2nd and 3rd strings simultaneously sounding all 3 strings.
I - Index plays the 3rd string.
R - Rasguedo - A flamenco strum. Strike the chord away from you, downward, with A, M and I in rapid succession.

RIGHT HAND POSITION FOR THE CLUSTER, ARPEGGIO AND ARPEGGIATED CLUSTER

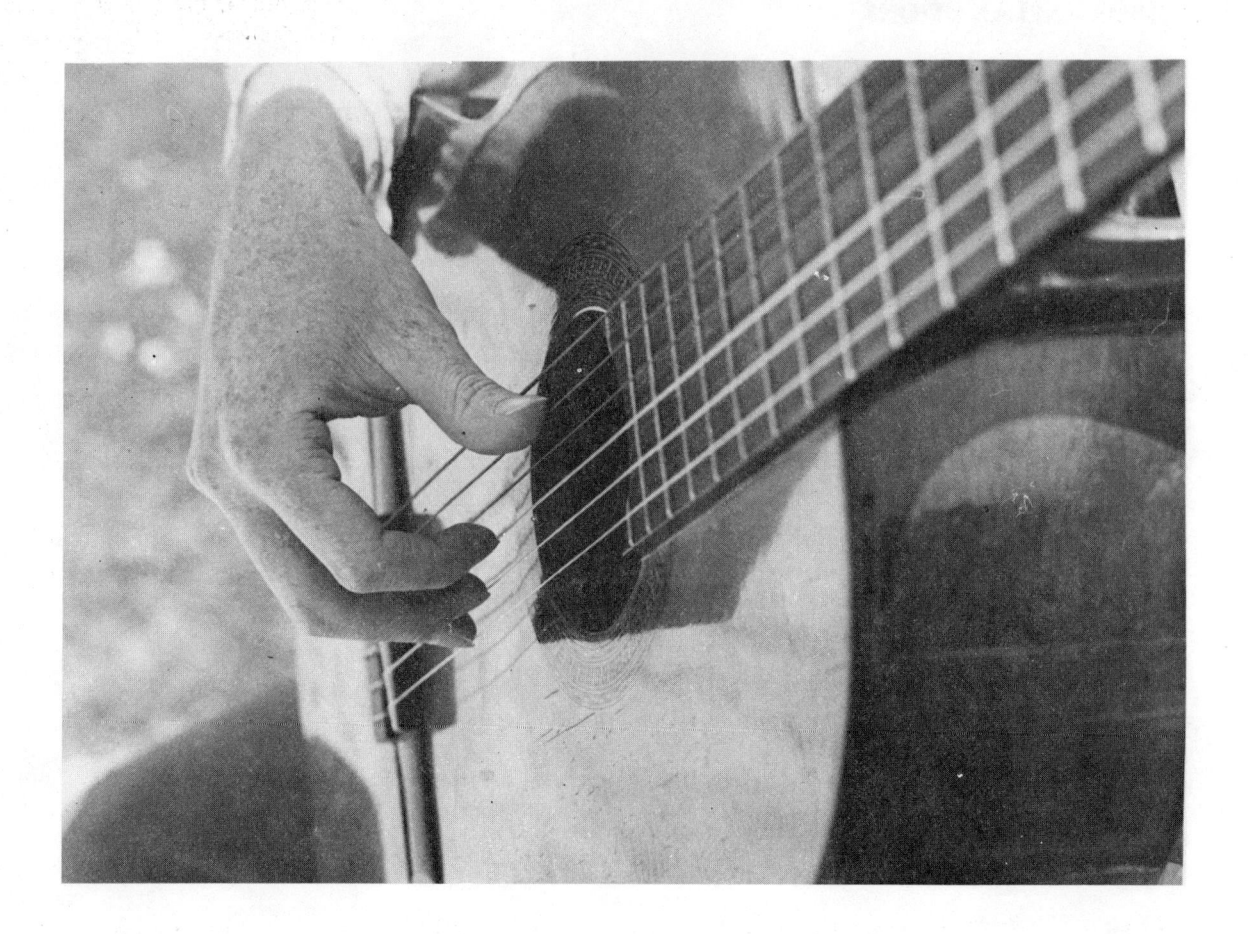

I, M, A (1st, 2nd and 3rd fingers) Sound the 3rd, 2nd and 1st strings

>Index Finger- 3rd string
>Middle Finger- 2nd string
>Anular (ring) Finger- 1st string

Your fingers should be placed on the underside of the string. The point of contact is under the fingernail, where the flesh and the nail meet. The thumb is extended away from the fingers and approaches the string from above.

Cluster strums: Thumb plucks the bass notes and the fingers pull the first 3 strings simultaneously.

Arpeggio: Thumb plucks the bass notes and fingers sound the 1st, 2nd and 3rd strings one at a time producing a "harp-like" and flowing sound.

Arpeggiated Cluster: P, plucks the bass notes. I-Index finger plays the 3rd string. M + A play the 1st and 2nd strings together.